PARTS OF A
WHOLE

Albatros

Hi! My name's Ada. I'm very inquisitive, and very orderly too. I like organizing and sorting the things around me.

I'm really interested in what makes up different things.

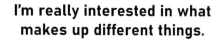

How about your lunch, for instance?
Have you ever thought about laying
all its different parts side by side?

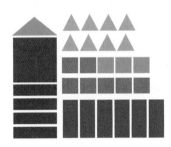

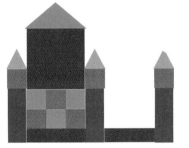

You haven't? That's a pity,
it's super fun! Come with me.
Let me show you how.

WHAT MAKES
A BOWL OF FRUIT SALAD?

tangerines

spoon

blackberries

grapes

strawberries

banana slices

pineapple

apple slices

kiwi

blueberries

bowl

honey

WHAT MAKES
A SANDBOX?

children

sand cakes

sand

toy trucks

toy cars

sand sifters

molds

insects

rakes

spades

nails

beams

ball

buckets

sandcastle

things left behind

WHAT MAKES
A CHRISTMAS TREE?

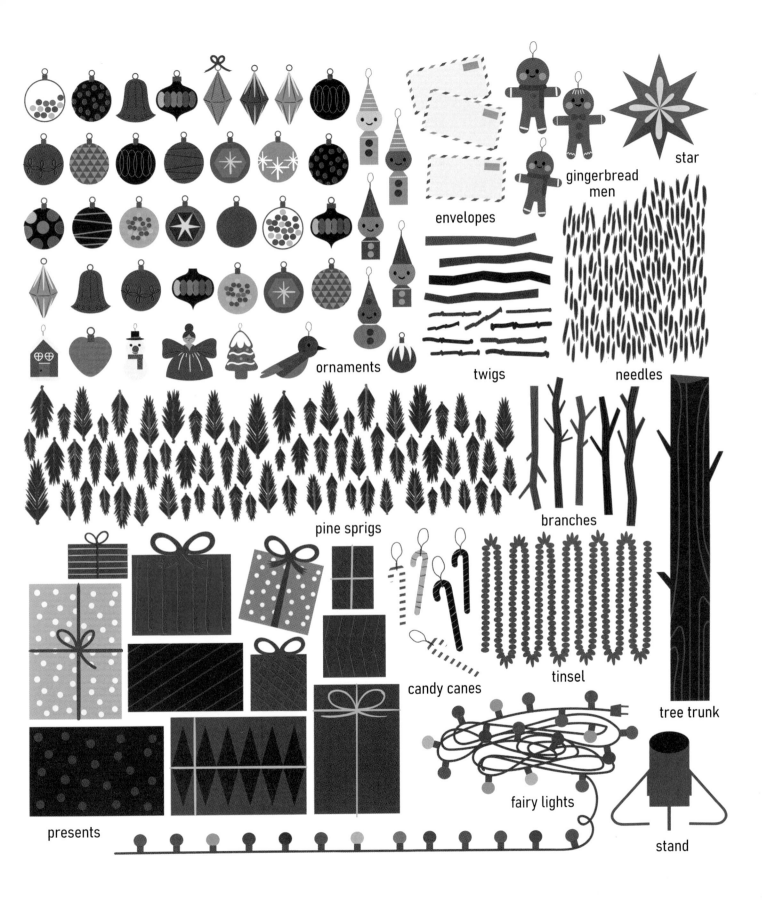

star

gingerbread men

envelopes

ornaments

twigs

needles

pine sprigs

branches

tree trunk

candy canes

tinsel

presents

fairy lights

stand

WHAT MAKES
A SWEET SHOP?

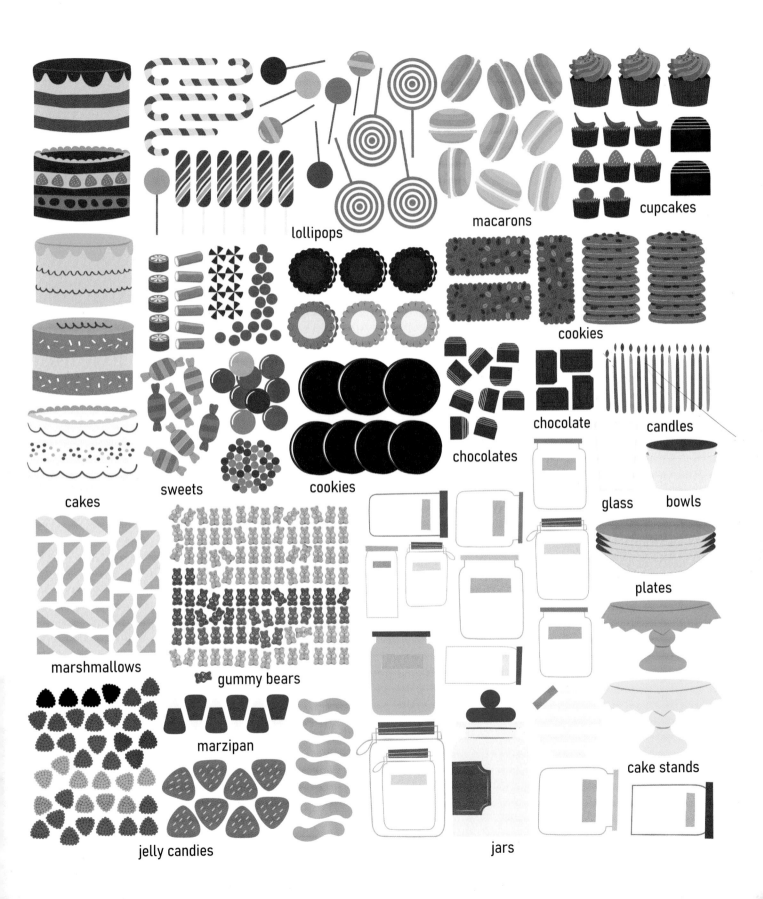

lollipops

macarons

cupcakes

cookies

chocolate

candles

chocolates

cookies

glass

bowls

sweets

plates

cake stands

cakes

marshmallows

gummy bears

marzipan

jars

jelly candies

WHAT MAKES
AN INTERSECTION?

bus

traffic cones

signals

cars

barrier

ice-cream truck

fire hydrant

bush

manhole cover

traffic signs

recycling bins

streetlamps

trees

bench

flowers

bicycles

pigeons

dog

people

WHAT MAKES
A HOCKEY MATCH?

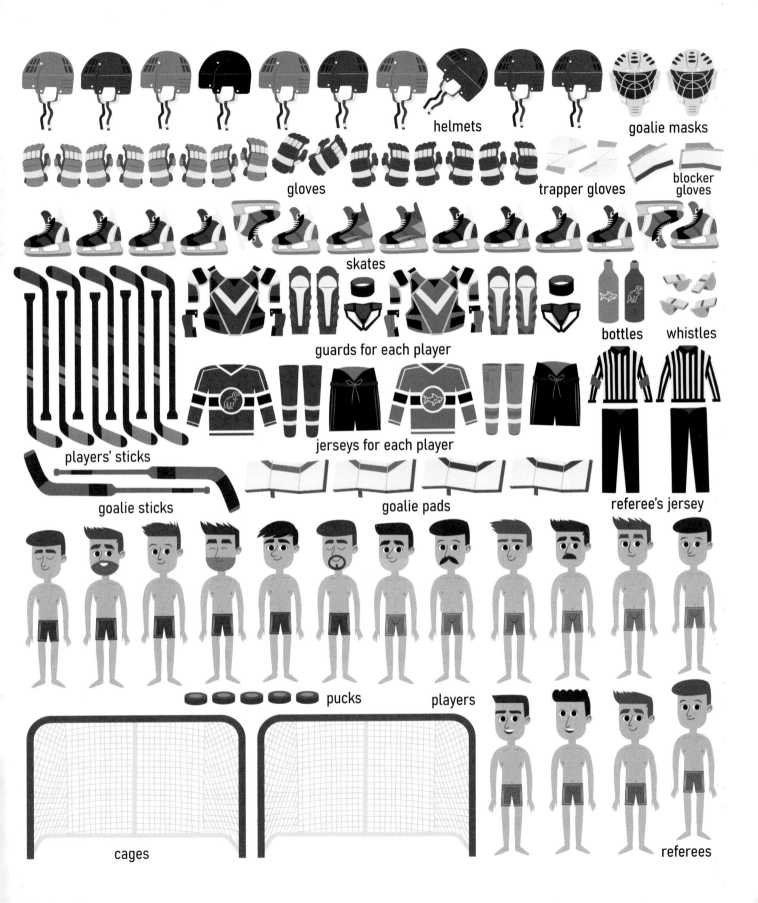

helmets

goalie masks

gloves

trapper gloves

blocker gloves

skates

guards for each player

bottles

whistles

players' sticks

jerseys for each player

referee's jersey

goalie sticks

goalie pads

pucks

players

cages

referees

WHAT MAKES
A CHAMBER ORCHESTRA?

harp

piano

clarinet

flute

cello

French horn

violin

double bass

bows

sheet music

chairs

music stands

stool

conductor

musicians

WHAT MAKES
A BOX OF CEREAL?

dried raisins

hazelnuts

dried figs

walnuts

almonds

rice puffs

seeds

dried coconut

cashews

dried apricots

O's

cereal box

flakes

WHAT MAKES
A CUCKOO CLOCK?

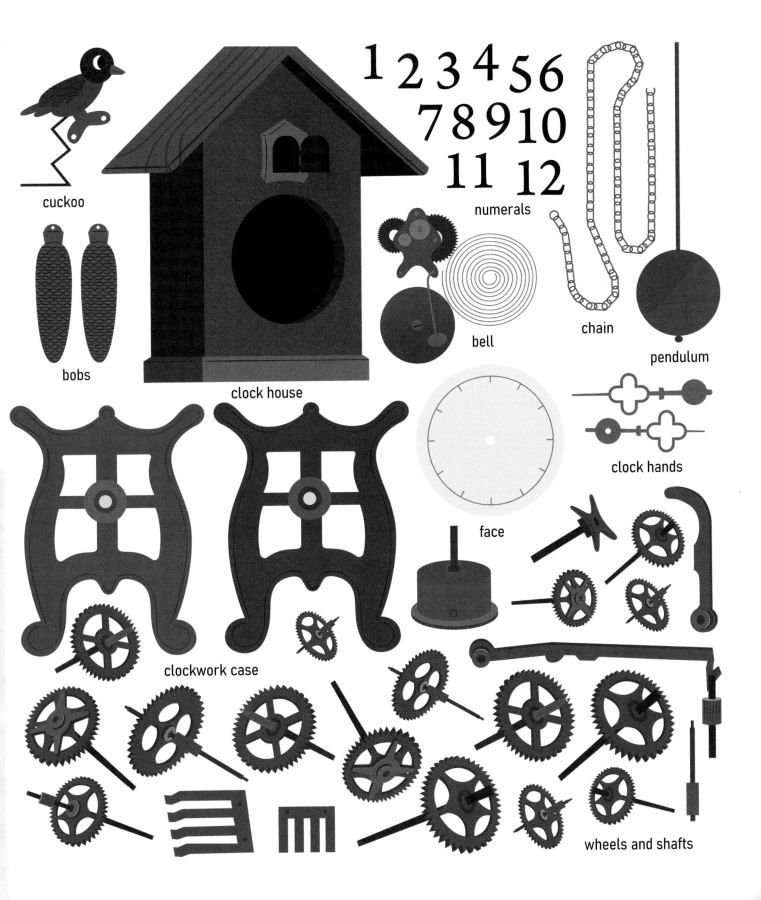

cuckoo

1 2 3 4 5 6
7 8 9 10
11 12

numerals

bobs

clock house

bell

chain

pendulum

face

clock hands

clockwork case

wheels and shafts

WHAT MAKES
A RAILWAY SET?

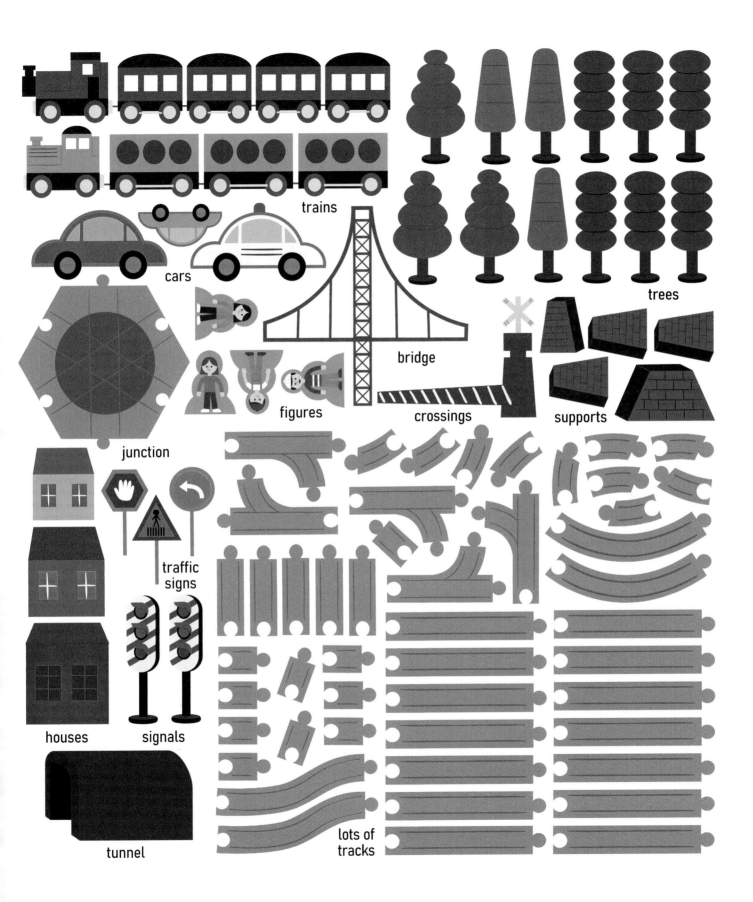

trains

trees

cars

bridge

crossings

supports

figures

junction

traffic
signs

houses

signals

tunnel

lots of
tracks

WHAT MAKES
A BOWL OF ALPHABET SOUP?

AAAAAAAAAABBBBBBBCCCCDDD
EEEEEEEFFFFFGGGGGGGHHHHH
IIIIIIIIIIJJJJJJJKKKKKKK
LLLLLLLLLMMMMMMMMNNNNOO
OOOOOPPPPPPPPPPPPPPQQQQQ
QQQRRRRRRRRRRSSSSSSSSSSS
TTTTTTTTTTTTTTTUUUUUUUUUU
VVVVVVVVVVVVVWWWWWXXX
XXXYYYYYYYYYYYZZZZZZZZZ

spaghetti letters

onions

carrots

water

salt

pepper

peas

herbs

leeks

bowl

celery

WHAT MAKES
A CYCLIST AND A BICYCLE?

tire pump

wheels

handlebars

mudguards

rack

bicycle frame

wallet

glasses

backpack

helmet

screws, nuts, and bolts

sprockets

saddle

gloves

bottle

map

chain

shoes

reflective vest

reflectors

rack

cyclist

cycling clothes

towel

cell phone

tools

basket

lamp

lock

lights

bell

pedals

WHAT MAKES
AN OAK TREE?

birds

leaves

branches

caterpillars

spiders

acorns

ants

centipedes

mushrooms

spider web

earthworms

ladybugs

tree trunk

roots

squirrels

beetles

WHAT MAKES
A BOUQUET OF FLOWERS?

flowers

pistils and stamens

seeds

ribbon

stems

leaves

petals

WHAT MAKES
A DOLLHOUSE?

pictures

car

stuffed animals

laptop

dolls

food

guitar

dishes

boxes

mirror

furniture

books

chandelier

bedding

plant

lamps

TV

table

refrigerator

bathtub

toilet

sink and faucet

radio

WHAT MAKES
AN AQUARIUM?

thermometer

starfish

water filter

heater

fish

water

shellfish and mussels

aquatic plants

sea urchins

pebbles

stones

castle

sand

branches

WHAT MAKES
A ROLL OF TOILET PAPER?

perforated sheets
of toilet paper

cardboard
roll

WHAT MAKES
SPACE?

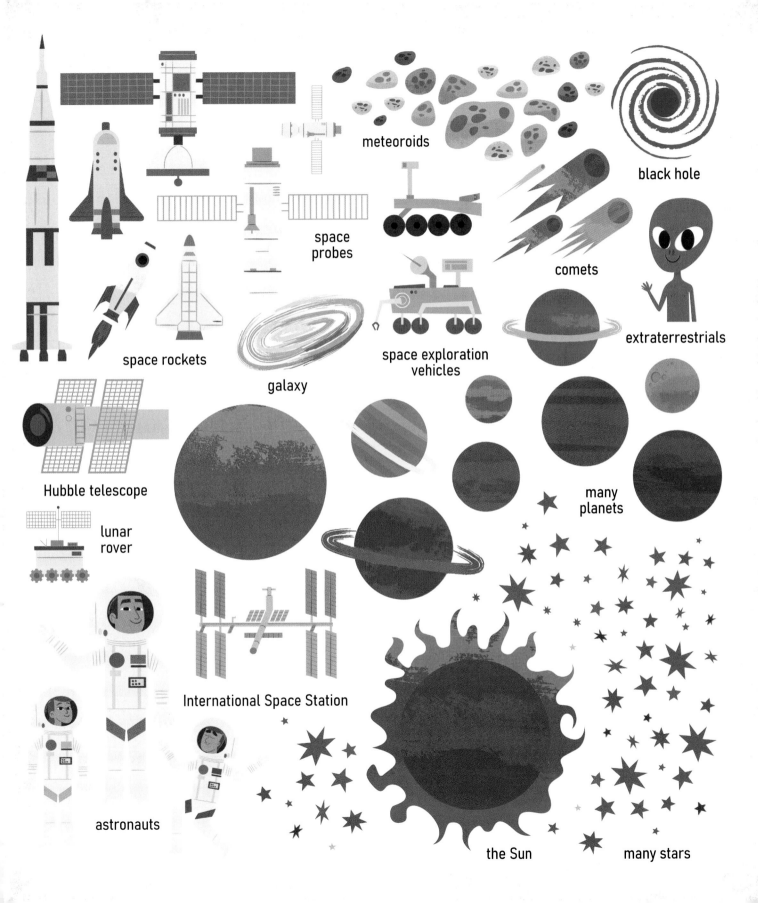

meteoroids

black hole

space probes

comets

extraterrestrials

space rockets

galaxy

space exploration vehicles

Hubble telescope

many planets

lunar rover

International Space Station

the Sun

many stars

astronauts

Will you show me all the things in your room?

© Designed by B4U Publishing for Albatros, an imprint of Albatros Media Group, 2022.
5. května 22, Prague 4, Czech Republic
Author: Magda Garguláková, Illustrator: © Federico Bonifacini
Printed in Ukraine by Unisoft.

ISBN: 978-80-00-06358-4